Remembering
Tallahassee

Andrew N. Edel

TURNER
PUBLISHING COMPANY

The Gallie-Munro Opera House was the focal point for community social affairs before 1900. Originally built by Alexander Gallie in 1874, Robert Munro bought it and renovated it twelve years later. It housed road shows, choir concerts, dance recitals, and school graduations. It has been restored to its 1890 appearance.

Remembering
Tallahassee

Turner Publishing Company
4507 Charlotte Avenue • Suite 100
Nashville, Tennessee 37209
(615) 255-2665

Remembering Tallahassee

www.turnerbookstore.com

Library of Congress Control Number: 2010923505

ISBN: 978-1-59652-635-8
ISBN-13: 978-1-68336-887-8 (pbk)

Printed in the United States of America

CONTENTS

ACKNOWLEDGMENTS...VII

PREFACE VIII

A CAPITAL BEGINNING
(1860s–1900) 1

A CAPITAL IDEA
(1901–1920) 49

A CAPITAL CITY
(1921–1940) 73

A CAPITAL COMPLEX
(1941–1970)..105

NOTES ON THE PHOTOGRAPHS 133

Added in 1902, the cupola on the new Capitol dome was the highest spot in Tallahassee and afforded great views of the area. This view, taken around 1914, shows the east side of Monroe Street and the Leon County Courthouse, with its tower.

ACKNOWLEDGMENTS

This volume, *Remembering Tallahassee,* is the result of the cooperation and efforts of many individuals and organizations. It is with great thanks that we acknowledge in particular the valuable contribution of the State Archives of Florida, Erik Robinson, and N. Adam Watson, Photographic Archivist at the archives.

This project represents countless hours of review and research. The researchers and writer have reviewed thousands of photographs. We greatly appreciate the generous assistance of the archives listed here, without whom this project could not have been completed.

The goal in publishing this work is to provide broader access to a set of extraordinary photographs. The aim is to inspire, provide perspective, and evoke insight that might assist officials and citizens, who together are responsible for determining Tallahassee's future. In addition, the book seeks to preserve the past with respect and reverence.

With the exception of touching up imperfections that have accrued with the passage of time and cropping where necessary, no changes have been made. The focus and clarity of many images are limited to the technology and the ability of the photographer at the time they were recorded.

We encourage readers to reflect as they explore Tallahassee, stroll along its streets, or wander its neighborhoods. It is the publisher's hope that in making use of this work, longtime residents will learn something new and that new residents will gain a perspective on where Tallahassee has been, so that each can contribute to its future.

—*Todd Bottorff, Publisher*

PREFACE

The photographic history of Tallahassee is well documented. At least four books of historic photographs have been published, thousands of images are available online at the State Archives, and many more have been included in other websites, articles, and videos. There are, however, compelling reasons for another book of historic photographs of Tallahassee. First, owing to the sheer number of extant photographs, even those familiar with the city's history will likely discover new images. Those unfamiliar with the city's past will reap a fresh glimpse into the rich photographic history of this community. Second, in addition to photographs, every book or portfolio offers its own commentary and perspective on the past. The focus of this volume is on Tallahassee's rich cultural heritage amid its lovely natural setting.

Individually, photographs offer an unspoiled glimpse of another place and time. Aided with informative text about specific elements, the viewer can draw his own insights and interpretation. As a collection, photographs constitute a history of a community's challenges, growth, and change. To help the viewer visually experience the historical continuity of Tallahassee, the images are arranged chronologically.

The materials used in developing the captions and overall perspective of the book are the product of many hours of research at the Florida State Library and Archives, Florida State University library, Supreme Court library, and Old Capitol collections.

Many in the general public have gained a cursory knowledge of Tallahassee in recent years. As the state capital of Florida, it is the setting for national news stories about the entire state. Every year thousands of people come to Tallahassee, some to attend the universities, others to work for the state government, and many as tourists to visit the state capital. For all those wishing to discover more about Tallahassee the goal of this work is to provide some insight and perspective about its traditions, history, people, and culture.

Summaries of each of the four eras provide historical background for the photographs. Section 1, A Capital Beginning, briefly describes the founding of the city, and spans the Civil War to the turn of the century. Section 2, A Capital Idea, covers the impact of education and government in the first two decades of the twentieth century. Section 3, A Capital City, traces the city's growth from a small rural town. Section 4, A Capital Complex, covers capital expansion from the beginning of World War II to the 1970s.

In each era the selection of photographs together with the captions and introduction provides a broad perspective on the development of Tallahassee. Various aspects are traced from period to period—the economy, civic improvements, education, state government, and social trends.

Tallahassee is situated in a garden spot of green hills, year-round flowers, and majestic oaks draped with Spanish moss. Walking around Tallahassee, one covers the same ground traversed by Apalachee Indians and Spanish conquistadors. Desoto, Osceola, Andrew Jackson, governors, presidents, slaves, and adventurers all walked the land. The origin of the Native American word *tallahassee* is generally translated "old fields" or "abandoned villages." Perhaps "ghost town" is a more apt translation, for it evokes the romanticism of Tallahassee—a city with a strong sense of its past in a timeless natural setting.

It is hoped that this work will add to the understanding of the unique cultural heritage of Tallahassee.

This rare mola was caught off St. Marks, Florida, and brought to Tallahassee on the back of a truck. Only 20 miles from the little fishing village of St. Marks, Tallahassee is close to the Gulf of Mexico. Fishing and water sports have long been a favorite pastime.

A Capital Beginning

(1860s–1900)

Although founded as the capital city of Florida, over a decade after the Civil War Tallahassee still looked like a frontier town, with few buildings and wide, rough dirt streets. Residents pose with a horse-drawn wagon in the middle of town on Monroe Street. The Phoenix building at right burned in 1877.

The wedding of Florence Holland and William Bull took place at Greenwood Plantation after the end of the Civil War in 1865. The bridegroom had just been mustered out of the Confederate army after being imprisoned for two years at Johnson's Island in Lake Erie. Bull sits at center with his bride on his right (the third person from left).

One of Tallahassee's oldest residences, the Columns was located on the southwest corner of Adams Street and Park Avenue. Built ca. 1830 and moved in 1971 to the northwest corner of Park Ave. and Duval St., it has served as private home, bank, boardinghouse, restaurant, library, and home of the chamber of commerce.

The Morgan Hotel on Adams Street across from the Capitol had many names and owners. Originally built in 1834 by Thomas Brown, who later became governor, it was first known as Brown's Inn. It was called the City Hotel in 1839, the Adelphi in 1840, and finally the Morgan Hotel. It was destroyed by fire in 1886.

This is the oldest known photograph of Florida's Old Capitol, probably the west side, between 1845 and 1870. The Greek Revival structure was designed by architect Cary W. Butt of Mobile, Alabama. Construction began in 1839, but funds ran out and it was not completed until 1845, when Florida became a state. The total cost was $55,000.

Outside an unkempt Capitol in 1875, Governor Marcellus Stearns, center front, greets Harriet Beecher Stowe, the lady in black on the sixth step. Mrs. Stowe, famous abolitionist author of *Uncle Tom's Cabin,* settled in Florida after the Civil War, where she helped establish schools for the children of former slaves.

The Grove was Tallahassee's most famous antebellum house. It was the residence of territorial governor Richard Keith Call from 1836 to 1839 and 1841 to 1844, and the thirty-third governor Leroy Collins from 1955 to 1961. Ellen Call Long, seated in the center, was the daughter of Governor Call. The house has remained in the Call family since the 1830s.

Produce and goods, many from the outlying farms and plantations, were sold fresh daily at this marketplace on Park Avenue, shown sometime in the 1870s. After emancipation, many former slaves in the area found themselves back working on the plantations, only now with contracts approved by the Freedman's Bureau.

In 1885, the Florida Railway and Navigation Company was consolidated from many north Florida railroad lines, some dating back to the old Tallahassee Railroad Company, chartered in 1835. This inspection team poses in front of an engine, originally of the Indiana, Peru and Chicago line, named the *C. B. Robinson*.

Governor William D. Bloxham entertains guests at his city residence. Elected in 1880, Bloxham, a Leon County resident, moved from his plantation southeast of Tallahassee to this house on Calhoun Street. With him are (left to right) George Lewis, Willie Bloxham, Mrs. Bloxham, Governor Bloxham, Mrs. George Lewis.

In 1888, the Flagg family and servants pose in front of their home on McCarty Street, later renamed Park Avenue. Originally built in 1840 by Captain Richard Shine purportedly with materials from the earlier territorial Capitol, it was remodeled in 1894 by the Chittenden family. The house has served as hospital, boardinghouse, and dining spot.

Florida's 14th governor Edward Aylsworth Perry (front center, hands clasped) and cabinet pause for a photograph on the Capitol steps in 1885. During his administration, Florida adopted a new constitution and established a state board of education. In October 1885, surprised Capitol visitors were greeted by an ostrich roaming the fenced grounds, a present to the governor.

Florida State University traces its beginnings to 1851 when the state legislature established the West Florida Seminary. The seminary officially opened in 1857 in this building, constructed by the city three years earlier on a site formerly known as Gallows Hill. The building was leveled in 1891 for the new College Hall.

Members of the 1885 Florida Senate gather on the Capitol steps for a group portrait. At right holding a coat is Secretary of the Senate William MacWilliams, and next to him, the lieutenant governor and president of the Senate Milton H. Mabry, later a Florida Supreme Court justice.

Tallahassee photographer Alvan Harper captured this image of two boys and crew of the Florida Railway and Navigation Company engine number 16. Harper's photograph reflects local pride felt toward the railroads—some of it owing to the presence of a railroad shop facility, the only industrial plant located in Tallahassee in the 1880s.

Landscaped with roses, hyacinths, and tulips, the Leon Hotel was a first-class hotel for a capital city. Also located at this prime site on Park Avenue was the first courthouse, which burned in 1879; the first Leon Hotel, burned in 1885; the second Leon Hotel, burned in 1925; and the post office, built in 1935.

The well-to-do of 1894 Tallahassee enjoyed many interesting diversions. Gathering for a fox hunt are members of three prominent estates and the local sheriff. Quail hunting became a profitable local business. The area is still considered a prime territory for quail hunting.

Members of the 1887 Florida legislature gather on the Capitol steps for a group portrait, dressed in three-piece suits, adorned with pocket watches, and wearing derby, bowler, and straw hats. A page boy stands in the front row.

Eight men of the Florida Cycling Club proudly show their penny-farthing bicycles. Tallahassee's well-to-do young men enjoyed this popular activity. In the back row are Captain Louis H. Strumm, at left, and Laurie A. Perkins, at right, who turn up in other photographs by Alvan Harper.

Another Alvan Harper photograph of four children and an adult on an ox cart, taken between 1885 and 1910. Harper's photographs show people at work and leisure, often outdoors at their home.

The sign behind the street-lamp reads "The Weekly Floridian—The Great Democratic Paper of Florida—One Dollar a Year." Established in 1829, it was one of the earliest newspapers in Florida. Through the *Floridian,* its editor and longtime owner, Charles E. Dyke, exerted a strong influence on public opinion and state legislation.

Alvan S. Harper lived in Tallahassee from 1884 until his death in 1911 and owned a photographic studio for most of that period. In 1946 some 2,000 glass negatives were discovered in the attic of Harper's former home. Now in the State Archives of Florida, the Harper Collection is a valuable resource on Tallahassee.

The Brokaw-McDougall House on North Meridian Street was built in the early 1850s for Perez Brokaw. His daughter Phebe married a Scottish immigrant, Alexander McDougall. After Phebe's death in 1883, Alexander married her sister Eliza. On the porch is Alexander McDougall with his children and wife Eliza, who holds an infant.

These laborers are boiling cane syrup. After the Civil War, the cotton economy never regained its prewar prosperity. Leon County farmers tried many alternative agricultural crops, including tobacco, nuts, pears, grapes, and sugar cane. The cane was cut and its juice squeezed out; the raw juice was then boiled into syrup in the large brick fireplace.

This sawmill is believed to have been on the Ochlocknee River, near Tallahassee. As mill fires increased, mills posted "No Smoking" signs, but most were ignored. One lumber mill superintendent noted in his diary, "Posted a sign in the mill according to instructions, 'No Smoking,' I had a lighted cigar in my mouth at the time."

Ox carts trudge down a wide Monroe Street. Economic prosperity motivated civic improvements during the 1880s and 1890s, including animal control and gas lamps (one is visible at left). A gas factory was built, pipes laid, and iron posts installed for the street-lamps. The gas lamps were turned on a few days before Christmas, 1888.

Members of the Winthrop and Merritt families ca. 1890. Mary the nurse, Matthew the coachman, and their son Eddie pose with Francis and Guy Winthrop (on horseback), descendants of a wealthy Massachusetts family. During Reconstruction, many blacks in Tallahassee found employment as servants to wealthy whites.

On Park Avenue ca. 1890, the Columns building is visible on the far left and the First Presbyterian Church, with scaffolding around the steeple, on the right. Around this time the ladies of the Tallahassee Improvement Association started a project to save "grand old shade trees, the noble oaks of Tallahassee."

John David Cay came to Tallahassee in the late 1800s with his wife, Georgia Winn, and family. He entered the turpentine and naval stores business, and later owned a livery stable. Advertising his livery stable is a parade entry, shown here, which consisted of a light carriage atop a heavy-duty wagon.

Tallahassee's old oaks, draped with Spanish moss, gracefully span the area's roads. These canopy roads, some following old Native American or Spanish trails, radiate from Tallahassee like spokes on a wheel. Once the source of goods and supplies coming from the plantations to Tallahassee, they are now designated scenic drives.

Erected for John G. Anderson in 1850, this house boasted Italian marble and French crystal chandeliers, and two double parlors. Napoleon Bonaparte Broward used it as the Governor's Mansion when he took office in 1905, until 1907. Bought by Allie Yawn Brown in the 1920s, it came to be known as the Brown House. Its leveling gave rise to the local preservation movement.

Three children with their toys pose in the yard for a portrait sometime in the late nineteenth century. Tallahassee children learned very early in life to avoid the spikes of the Spanish bayonet plant—behind the little girl at right. An interested onlooker reclines in a hammock on the porch at left.

John Fowler's family and company pause for a group portrait on the steps of the Capitol in 1893. Improvements following Harriet Beecher Stowe's visit almost twenty years earlier are noticeable. Renovations to the building, in 1891, included a new roof with added cupola, water closets, fountains, and fresh whitewash.

Lively's corner, at the southwest corner of Monroe and College, was originally built in 1875 as Lively's drugstore. In 1892 the popular Leon Bar operated as liquor store, bar, and pool room, and was a target of temperance advocates. It closed when the town went dry in 1904, and was later opened as another drugstore and as an office building.

Although it had a rough appearance, Ball Bros. and DeMilly general store was at the center of Tallahassee's business district on Monroe Street in the 1890s. The DeMilly family is one of Tallahassee's oldest, tracing its lineage back to Charles DeMilly, a soldier in the Napoleonic wars who immigrated to Tallahassee in 1828.

A source of community pride, the Tallahassee Railroad Company's mule-drawn trolley operated from 1889 to 1896. Two small red mules, Napoleon and Bucephalus, seen with a horse, had to be unhitched and hooked up to the opposite end of the car to begin its return run. The drivers would often wait for patrons to do their shopping.

Winburn's Restaurant advertises "Oysters" beside the ornate M. Lively drugstore on Monroe Street in 1894. Sidewalks were a constant problem. Many complained about stores blocking sidewalks with displays of merchandise. The U.S. Postal Service refused service until "good sidewalks were provided."

State Treasurer James B. Whitfield sits behind his desk at the Capitol, probably with his office staff. He later served as State Attorney General, then on the Supreme Court bench for almost forty years as one of Florida's most distinguished justices. The fireplace was sealed over in 1902 and used as a support for the new Capitol dome.

Young cyclists stop to pose for their photograph in December 1898. The smaller-wheeled bicycles were much easier to control than the high-wheeled penny-farthings.

Alvan S. Harper, in customary hat, long-sleeve shirt, and boots, attempts to photograph two dogs in a horse-drawn cart with, it appears, an early hand-held camera. Question is, who is photographing the photographer? The open longleaf pine and wiregrass habitat is typical of the area surrounding and to the north of Tallahassee.

College Hall was constructed in 1891 then replaced with the Westcott building in 1909. The school held several names in the span of a few years, from West Florida Seminary to Florida State College in 1901, Florida Female College in 1905, and Florida State College for Women in 1909.

Most of Tallahassee turned out to see and greet President McKinley and the First Lady during their visit in 1899, including "Dirty Smith" riding on an ox. Presidents Nixon, Carter, Clinton, and George H. W. Bush have also paid formal visits to the state capital.

Using locally grown tobacco, the Wanish Cigar Factory employed Cuban-born cigar maker Manuel Roffe, at far-left, to train the other workers. The cigar factory closed around the time the city went "dry," leading to rumors that the employees would not work in a town without liquor.

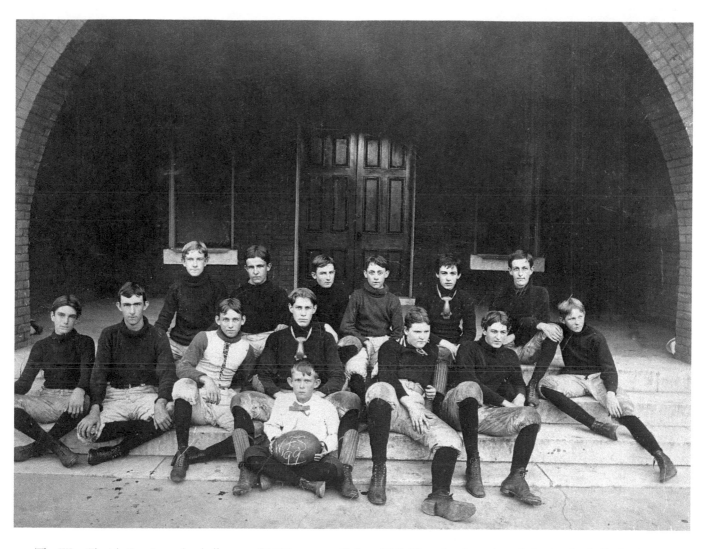

The West Florida Seminary football team of 1899 poses at College Hall. The school continued playing football after becoming Florida State College in 1901. F.S.C. won state championships in 1904 and 1905, coached by college president Albert Murphree. The college team wore purple and gold uniforms.

William Cabot Hodges, standing at right, served in the Florida Senate from 1922 to 1940 and was elected Senate President in 1935. "Homestead Bill" supported a homestead tax exemption amendment, aid for the blind, welfare for children, and pensions for the aged. His Tallahassee home, Goodwood Plantation, is now a museum.

On February 13, 1899, the frozen fountain on the Capitol grounds attested to the coldest temperature in Florida's history, at two degrees Fahrenheit below zero. It has snowed only 32 times in Tallahassee since 1891, with a one-day record of 2.8 inches on February 12, 1958. The area averages 35 days a year with minimum temperatures at, or below, freezing.

Known locally as "Gophers, Frogs, and Alligators," the Georgia, Florida & Alabama Railway ran 180 miles from Richland, Georgia, through Tallahassee to the Gulf Coast. During World War II it transported thousands of soldiers to Camp Gordon Johnson at Carrabelle. The Seaboard Air Line Railway took control of the line in 1928.

A Capital Idea

(1901–1920)

Mary Shutan, a 1902 Florida State College graduate, is fifth from the left in the front row in this "School of the South" class portrait from ca. 1900. In 1902 the co-ed student body numbered 252, and the school offered degrees in classical, literary, and scientific studies and a master of arts degree.

Boys with bikes and a horse-drawn buggy meet at a local crossroads. The canopied roads have shaped Tallahassee's growth and continue to influence the city. Originally transportation routes connecting the large plantations to town, the old moss-covered roadways later gave rise to residential and business areas.

In 1900, the town's first view of an automobile created a great deal of interest. John P. Brown, Sr., on the left next to the automobile, owned this Ford and Overland automobile dealership on Monroe Street, one of the first in town. Baxter Willis Brown, on the right, later operated a Studebaker dealership at the same location.

Governor William S. Jennings and cabinet pose at the start of the 1902 Capitol additions. Left to right in the foreground are Comptroller A. C. Croom, Governor Jennings, Attorney General William B. Lamar, Treasurer James B. Whitfield, Superintendent of Public Instruction William N. Sheats, and Agriculture Commissioner Benjamin E. McLin.

George W. Saxon, left, with hat, decided to switch from dry goods to banking, receiving a charter for the Capital City Bank in 1895. By the end of June, Capital City Bank reported total deposits of $41,000 and total resources of $84,000. In 1917, Capital City Bank approved a loan to the City of Tallahassee for $10,000.

The only Confederate capital east of the Mississippi not captured during the Civil War, Tallahassee joined the South in revering the Confederacy in the early twentieth century. Confederate battle flags were displayed in the Capitol, former soldiers and widows were granted pensions, and Confederate veterans were honored.

Inside the T. B. Byrd grocery store around 1905. Thomas Blake Byrd, fourth from right, and his wife, far right, often held receptions when offering a new line of groceries. Their daughter Kate, the taller girl in the photo, recalled her mother serving olives, pickles, cookies, and coffee, and decorating the store with vines and flowers.

By 1905 Tallahassee had its first fire department. Those aboard the first hose wagon, in front of the Leon County courthouse, include Willie McIntosh, Chief John Hamlin, Assistant Chief W. P. Phillips, and Eugene Levy. Dick and Jake are the horses. Before the department existed, a fire was once put out by two drugstore soda fountains.

Seated in a 1903 Panhard automobile, not to be mistaken for a Packard, are Zach Fenn, Phelps Wilson, and John P. Brown, Sr. The first cars in Tallahassee were novelty items, attracting attention, and the first city speed limit was 10 M.P.H. One early motorist noted, "To start an auto, the easiest thing was to get a group of people to push it for you and 'pop' the clutch."

The Florida State College graduating class of 1905 was the first class to wear caps and gowns. Also that year, the school became Florida Female College under the Buckman Act, which reorganized Florida's educational system. It would not have another co-ed class until 1947.

Until 1907 Florida's governors had to purchase or rent a home. Orion C. Parker, Jr., left, and his older brother, Robert C., ride atop a column en route to the site of the first Governor's Mansion. Built by the boys' father, Orion C. Parker, Sr., at a cost of $25,000 on the plans of Jacksonville architect Henry Klutho, the mansion boasted 24 huge columns.

Governor Napoleon B. Broward, his family, and sister-in-law Elsie Douglass, far right, pose on the steps of the new executive mansion. Elizabeth Broward, sitting on her mother's lap, was the first child born to an incumbent governor. Mrs. Broward selected the furnishings at a cost of $4,444.75. The mansion was demolished in 1955.

According to local tradition, chicken salad was often served at the many church bazaars and dinners on the grounds of the First Presbyterian church. The recipe has been handed down from Mrs. John Gamble for generations and is known as "Tallahassee Chicken Salad."

Using the state's large pine forests, the Florida lumber industry produced up to 7,000,000 gallons of turpentine and 800,000 barrels of rosin annually. A turpentine still near Tallahassee distilled turpentine and rosin from the crude gum harvested from pine trees.

The long-standing Florida State University and University of Florida football rivalry dates to this 1902 team. That year Florida State College, now FSU, twice played Florida Agricultural College, now UF. Each team won on their home field 6-0. On this team is Guyte P. McCord, later clerk of the Florida Supreme Court.

Lizzie Clemons stands on the porch of the Breeze Hotel, a boardinghouse she managed. She later married Madison Leslie, a legislator from Madison who had stayed at the house. While the Florida Legislature was in session, many families turned their large stately homes into boardinghouses.

Just two years after the Boy Scouts were founded in the United States, Tallahassee had its own troop. Standing on the left is Scout Master Will Yon. Among the others pictured are, seated second from right, Walter Phillips, and on the far right, John Christian. In 1912 a local paper reported that "the Boy Scout movement in Tallahassee is a sure thing."

Former governor William D. Bloxham lies in state in the governor's suite at the Capitol. He died on March 15, 1911. During the restoration of the governor's suite in the early 1980s, this photograph was sent to the Jet Propulsion Laboratory in California for digital imaging in order to reproduce the carpet seen underneath the casket.

Kate Byrd, far right, is pictured with the Leon Academy girls basketball team in 1914. This is one of a group of photographs documenting her life growing up in Tallahassee. She was born in 1898 to Thomas and Rubie Byrd. Other photographs of her include her father's grocery store, her family's home, a trip to Lake Bradford, and her portrait as Queen of the May Day festival.

Fanny Tiers bought Goodwood in 1911, made changes to the main house, and added the first swimming pool in Tallahassee, which she opened to the community. By 1925 the estate included the main house, seven guest cottages, two stables, a carriage house, skating rink, swimming pool, aviary, greenhouse, and a water tower.

By the 1920s brick streets and automobiles had replaced dirt roads and ox carts along Monroe Street. Electric lamps, benches, and street signs were welcomed improvements. The arrow seems to point to the one-story Capital City Bank. The two buildings on either side of the bank were built after 1900 when the city enjoyed a period of economic growth.

John P. Brown drives Mr. Lewis in a Maxwell touring car, decorated for a parade. They are outside the Ford dealership on Pensacola Street. Two years earlier, in 1912, Tallahassee first paved its streets, which the local paper heralded as "one of the greatest events in the history of Tallahassee."

During World War I, thousands of soldiers passed through Tallahassee on trains headed to ports or training camps. This visiting army plane sparked excitement and added to the growing interest in aviation. The first airstrip was Smith field off of St. Augustine Road about a mile from the Capitol.

A Capital City

(1921–1940)

A student competes in the shot put at the 1920 field day at Florida State College for Women. The college divided intramural teams between the "evens" classes graduating in even years, and the "odds" classes graduating in odd years. Events included baseball, basketball, high jump, long jump, hurdles, running, and javelin.

Revenue agent James E. Bowdoin stands beside a Model-T Ford with a confiscated moonshine still in downtown Tallahassee. During the Prohibition era, moonshine stills were abundant in the area west of the city. Bowdoin was shot in West Florida in 1925. Leon County was dry from 1904 to 1967.

Tallahassee grandly celebrated its centennial with a week of parades, shows, fireworks, concerts, and exhibits from November 9 to 15, 1924. The Knights of Columbus float participated in the centennial celebration parade on November 11. The "Black Citizens Historical Parade" was held separately.

Among the firefighters on the truck at a gas station is Fire Chief Thomas P. Coe holding young Ridgeway Coe. By 1924 Tallahassee's fire department had three paid full-time men and 20 partly paid "volunteers." The equipment consisted of two triple combination motor-driven pumpers carrying 1,200 feet of hose.

The Middle Florida Ice Company was located near Gaines Street and next to the railroad to allow freight needing refrigeration to be quickly unloaded and stored in special coolers. Although electric service was available in 1908, as of the 1920s few Tallahassee residents had electric refrigerators and the ice man was still a familiar figure.

Students at Florida State College for Women pose as firemen on a fire truck at the Tallahassee Fire Department. The photograph was taken around 1925 at the fire department located in the City Hall building. Just five years earlier, a Sunday morning fire destroyed East Hall at the college.

The Carnegie Library building is currently the oldest building at Florida A&M University and houses the Black Archives Research Center and Museum. Financed with the assistance of a $10,000 grant from philanthropist Andrew Carnegie and completed in 1907, it was the first library funded by Carnegie on a black university campus.

Colonel Thomas Jefferson Appleyard, veteran of the Confederate Navy, speaks during the ceremony for the return of the regimental colors of the 4th Florida Infantry in September 1927. The flag was captured at the Battle of Franklin, Tennessee, November 30, 1864, by Charles McCleary of the 111th Ohio Volunteer Infantry.

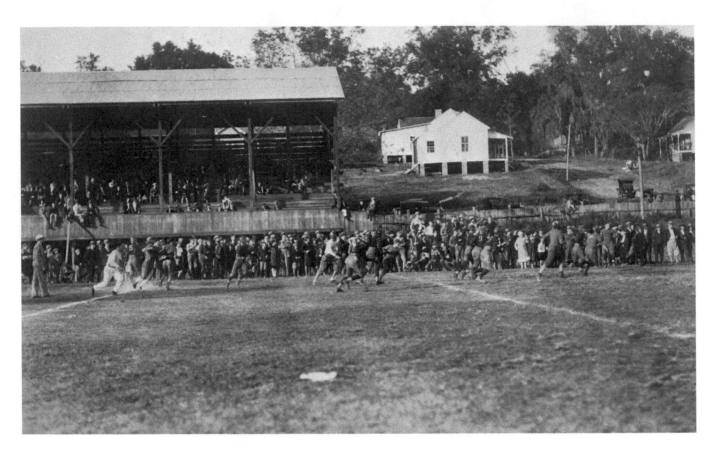

A 1920s Leon High School football team plays at Centennial Field on South Monroe. Started in 1916, Leon Football was the winningest high school program in Florida in the twentieth century, with 535 wins, 61 winning seasons, 3 state championships, 3 state runner-ups, and 12 national high school records.

Florida's Democratic governor John W. Martin, on the right holding his hat, greets New York's governor Al Smith, the 1928 Democratic candidate for President. Smith did not carry Florida in the election, for several reasons. He opposed Prohibition, and Republican Herbert Hoover was popular in Florida for his humanitarian work following two major hurricanes.

In 1913, the Florida Supreme Court moved into a new building, where it shared space with the Railroad Commission. When the court moved to its own building in 1949, the building was renamed the Whitfield. The court furniture, saved when the Whitfield Building was leveled in the 1970s, was placed back inside the Old Capitol.

Organized before the Civil War, the First Baptist Church of Tallahassee dedicated its second building in November 1915. Under pastor-builder J. Dean Adcock, the church purchased a lot on the northeast corner of Adams Street and College Avenue for $5,000 and built this new church, seating 350.

The first Masonic lodge was built on this site in 1854 and was replaced with this Masonic Hall in 1929. It was used until the 1970s when it became the Governor's Club. As Florida's first Masonic lodge, the lodge performed the cornerstone ceremonies for the 1845 State Capitol building.

The dedication ceremonies of Dale Mabry Municipal Airport lasted two days, November 10-11, 1929. Governor Doyle Carlton dedicated the town's first airport, complete with a hangar, gas service station, and lighting system. The field was named for Dale Mabry, a World War I aviator killed in a dirigible crash in 1922.

Victor and John Camechis owned and operated the Venetia Restaurant and Hotel located on the northeast corner of Adams Street and College Avenue. Opened in 1929, the business burned December 6, 1933. John Camechis, from the island of Patmos, was the first known immigrant of Greek heritage living in Tallahassee.

Florida's 25th governor, Doyle E. Carlton, and members of his cabinet sit for the photographer in a meeting room at the State Capitol. During Carlton's administration, 1929 to 1933, Florida faced four disasters: collapse of the state's land boom, a violent hurricane, Mediterranean fruitfly infestation, and the national Depression.

This gymnasium building at Florida Agricultural and Mechanical College for Negroes was a project of the Federal Emergency Relief Administration, a New Deal program. Founded in 1887, this historically black school became Florida Agricultural and Mechanical University in 1953.

Beers Construction Company built the U.S. Post Office and Federal Courthouse at a cost of $300,000. A Works Progress Administration project, it opened January 14, 1937, on Park Avenue at the old Leon Hotel site. Edward Buk Ulreich, a Hungarian-born artist, painted the murals in the lobby depicting the history of Florida.

The national crime wave of the 1930s struck Tallahassee on January 29, 1934, when Sheriff Frank Stoutamire, tipped off about a bank robbery, pursued two suspects in a sedan onto Adams Street. Racing past the Furniture Exchange, officer Barney Gatlin shot out the tire of the fleeing car. One of the suspects was wounded during the arrest.

This typical 1930s grocery store, owned by John L. Jordan, at right, was at 519 Gaines Street just a few blocks from the train station. Once a mixed residential neighborhood, the city voted in 1925 to allow businesses to locate near the train depot without the consent of area residents.

Architect M. Leo Elliot designed, and the Beers Construction Company built, two new wings to the State Capitol. Construction started in 1936 on the north chamber, for the House of Representatives, and was finished the next year. The south wing, for the Senate, was delayed by World War II and not completed until 1947.

The *Tallahassee Flyer*, a streamlined motor coach owned by the Seaboard Air Line Railway, stops on its inaugural run from Jacksonville. Greeting it are Governor David Sholtz, several justices of the Supreme Court, and the state railroad commissioner. Mrs. Sholtz, with the flowers, christened the train with a bottle of wine.

A new and larger State Theatre opened on College Avenue less than a year after the original burned in 1933. The Art Deco theater included a marquee that reached across the entire front of the building, and a two-story-tall vertical sign. It closed in 1971 and was demolished in 1988.

The inauguration of Governor Frederick Preston Cone takes place on the steps of the Capitol on January 5, 1937. On the podium is Secretary of State Robert A. Gray holding a document, Governor Cone, and behind them former governor Dave Sholtz. Chief Justice James B. Whitfield, seated directly behind the U.S. flag, administered the oath.

Proud members of the Tallahassee Police Department stand beside their vehicles around 1937. Established in 1841, it is the oldest police department in the South, third oldest police department in the nation, and the third-longest accredited law enforcement agency in the United States.

Present on October 10, 1938, at the first scheduled Eastern Airlines flight from Tallahassee, are Mayor J. R. Jinks, second from left, and president of Eastern Airlines, Captain Eddie Rickenbacker, fourth from left. Eastern Airlines offered four daily flights from Tallahassee to Memphis, Tennessee, Birmingham, and Montgomery, Alabama.

Genevieve Beadel and party are ready for a dove shoot at Tall Timbers Plantation in January 1938. A 1931 report of research on the effects of fire on wildlife at Tall Timbers established that annual controlled fires were critical for clearing the underbrush and maintaining the quail population.

The 1939 May Day Queen and King pose with their court under the majestic May Oak in Lewis Park. One of the oldest festivals in the South, more than 130 May Queens were crowned in this annual pageant, the last one in 1974. For years, the May Queen and her court changed into their costumes at the Knott House. The May Oak collapsed in August 1986.

Popular in the 1930s, the Green Derby nightclub and restaurant operated until the 1950s, later becoming the Country Flower Shop. It literally sits on the other side of the tracks, just south of the Monroe Street railroad overpass. In 2006 a church purchased the property and started remodeling it as an office and coffeehouse.

Members of Florida State College for Women Astronomy Club assemble for a portrait around 1940. With a number of excellent professors on the science and math faculties, the science department at F.S.C.W. boasted four science laboratories: biology, chemistry, physics, and psychology.

The Army Air Corps leased Dale Mabry Field from the city in 1941 for a training base. Barracks, repair shops, a warehouse, and a hospital were added. More than seven thousand men trained at the base, including Filipino, British, Chinese, French, and Brazilian airmen. After the base closed in late 1945, the city retained all of the base facilities.

A Capital Complex

(1941–1970)

Luella Knott, sitting to the far right, hosts a bridal luncheon in her dining room in 1948. The dining room has changed very little—visitors to the Knott House museum can see the same table, chandelier, and mirrors, even the very china and tablecloth.

Couples say goodnight in front of Bryan Hall at Florida State College for Women. The city provided chaperoned dances and parties with food and entertainment for the soldiers from Dale Mabry Air Field. The Victorettes, the Bombadiers, the Girls Defense Club, and other clubs were formed to provide dates and dance partners.

Ivan Munroe, "the father of aviation in Tallahassee," stands beside the door of an experimental seaplane at the city airport in 1946. Munroe, the airport manager, later provided flight training, aerial photography, and charter services. Surviving six crashes, he was quoted as saying, "In my day the men were made of steel and the planes were made of wood."

A National Airlines DC-6 is being serviced at the Tallahassee airport on September 1, 1947. With the departure of the Army air base, civilian air traffic reopened after the war. National Airlines provided service to Jacksonville, Pensacola, Mobile, and New Orleans. National's slogan was "the Buccaneer Route."

Lee Hall, the administration building at Florida A&M University, was named in honor of President John Robert Edward Lee, Sr. During his administration, from 1924 to 1944, President Lee expanded the physical plant, built a stronger faculty, and extended services. Florida A&M is home to the world-famous "Marching 100" band.

Tallahassee experienced a boom after World War II, the population growing almost 70 percent by 1950. In view here, facing north on Monroe Street, is the central business district. Butler's shoes is on the left, the 1928 Exchange Bank building is in back at right, and the trees on the right stand in front of the Leon County Court House.

Florida governor Millard Caldwell greets General Jonathan Wainwright, May 30, 1947. General Wainwright was forced to surrender U.S. forces in the Philippines to Japan in 1941. He was a prisoner of war until 1945, when he returned home to a hero's welcome and was awarded the Medal of Honor. He retired from active duty in August 1947.

A Southeastern Telephone Company traffic operating room as seen in 1949, with long-distance switchboards on the left and local lines on the right. The first telephone exchange opened in Tallahassee in 1896 with 65 subscribers. Operators had to be unmarried women between 17 and 26, and able to reach the top of the switchboard.

On January 4, 1949, crowds gather in front of the Seven Seas restaurant on Monroe Street for Fuller Warren's inauguration day activities. A large parade was followed by the swearing-in ceremonies, then a picnic on the Capitol grounds with 28,000 plates of barbecue, and finally an inaugural ball in the evening.

In the 1950s Monroe Street remained the central business district. From the left are Fain drugstore, Gulf Life Insurance Company, the Book Corner, and Jenkins Music Company. From 1910 to 1950, Fain's drugstore was informally known as the "information" center of Tallahassee.

After World War II the impact of veterans applying to colleges on the G.I. Bill was a leading factor in Florida State College for Women becoming co-ed as Florida State University in 1947. Participating in the 1950 FSU homecoming parade, the "Veterans of Former Wars" are alumni of the 1902–1905 Florida State College football team.

Although national prohibition ended in 1933, Leon County continued to be a "dry" county, prohibiting anything stronger than beer and wine until 1967. With many legislators coming from "wet" counties, Tallahasseans found ways to oblige them. In 1953 beverage agents in Tallahassee inspect confiscated bottles.

By 1955, the Florida Governor's Mansion on Adams Street had developed severe structural problems and was scheduled for demolition. On July 28, a large crowd was on hand for the start of the Executive Mansion's auction, led by auctioneer Howard Cranston. It was announced that "the auction will go on until everything is sold."

By the 1950s and 1960s the civil rights movement in Tallahassee had started protests and boycotts in attempts to end the segregation laws in place since the early twentieth century. On March 16, 1960, civil rights protesters attempted a boycott against the Mecca, a popular diner across from Florida State University.

A fire destroys a Frenchtown home in the 1950s. An older neighborhood, by the 1920s Frenchtown was established as a thriving African-American community. Before integration, many visiting musicians, such as Ray Charles, played at Frenchtown's cafes or stayed at its hotels while working the "Chitlin' Circuit."

A man and three boys stop along a garden walk at McClay Gardens. In 1923 Alfred McClay purchased the site and started an extensive ornamental garden featuring camellias, azaleas, dogwoods, a secret garden, and a reflecting pool. His widow donated it to the state in 1953. In 1965 the garden was renamed in McClay's honor.

Inaugural parades traditionally came down Monroe Street to the Capitol. On his way to the reviewing stand, Governor Collins waves to the crowds on January 4, 1955. Governor Collins' moderate positions on racial issues slowly led the state toward integration, and he strengthened Florida's educational system.

Guests tour the recently completed Governor's Mansion during the 1957 inauguration ceremonies. Work commenced in 1955 on the new mansion, designed after Andrew Jackson's home in Nashville, the Hermitage. During construction, Governor Collins moved next door to "the Grove," his wife's family home since territorial days.

Florida State University students walking to classes view snow on the palm trees, Spanish moss, and the old Westcott building, an unusual sight. On February 12–13, 1958, Tallahassee was hit with the heaviest snowfall on record in a 24-hour period—2.8 inches. It has snowed only 32 times in Tallahassee since 1891.

On May 26, 1956, two Florida A&M University students refused to give up their bus seats and were arrested. African Americans then started a bus boycott. On December 24, C. K. Steele and Dan Speed rode in the "white" section of a Tallahassee bus, ending the boycott. On January 7, 1957, the city repealed the bus segregation regulation.

Civil rights protesters, many of them students from Florida A&M University, let their signs make their point during a December 1960 boycott and picketing of downtown Tallahassee stores. The protests were designed to point out the lack of progress in desegregating the lunch counters at downtown stores.

Students try a new diet at the cafeteria at Leonard A. Wesson Elementary School in 1961, located near a new subdivision. It opened as Prince Murat school at Dale Mabry Field in 1946, was moved and renamed South City School in 1949, and finally renamed after Leonard Wesson, a former School Board member, in 1956.

Since its founding in 1824, Tallahassee has survived many attempts to relocate the Capitol. Throughout the years, the city has responded by taking measures to retain the Capitol. This business district along Monroe Street was leveled to make way for the State House of Representatives office building in the 1970s.

Miccosukee Seminole tribal leaders present William Kidd, an engineer for the state, with a colorful Indian jacket on the steps of the State Capitol on October 16, 1961, as a memento for being given enough state land for a commercial development. Left to right are Stanley Frank, Jimmie Tiger, John Poole, John Willie, William Kidd, Tommy Tiger, Calvin Sanders, and Buffalo Tiger.

Governor and Mrs. Haydon Burns ride in the inaugural parade with Adjutant General Henry W. McMillan to the reviewing stand. Burns served as Florida's governor from January 5, 1965, to January 3, 1967. Governor Burns had a short term because the cycle of gubernatorial elections was changed so that it would not fall on presidential election years.

Governor Claude Kirk meets with Florida State University coach Bill "Pete" Peterson and the football team in September 1969. Coach Peterson, with a young Bobby Bowden on his staff, brought a young football program into national college football prominence, a tradition later continued by Bobby Bowden as head coach at FSU.

Notes on the Photographs

These notes, listed by page number, attempt to include all aspects known of the photographs. Each of the photographs is identified by the page number, a title or description, photographer and collection, archive, and call or box number when applicable. Although every attempt was made to collect all data, in some cases complete data may have been unavailable due to the age and condition of some of the photographs and records.

II   GALLIE-MUNRO OPERA HOUSE
State Archives of Florida
rc02075

VI   VIEW FROM THE CAPITOL
State Archives of Florida   rc02421

X   MOLA ON A TRUCK
State Archives of Florida   GE1759

2   HORSE-DRAWN WAGON
State Archives of Florida
Rc09760

3   WEDDING OF FLORENCE HOLLAND
State Archives of Florida
PR11861

4   THE COLUMNS
State Archives of Florida
PR12009

5   MORGAN HOTEL
State Archives of Florida
Rc03612

6   OLD CAPITOL
State Archives of Florida
Rc00569

7   GOVERNOR STEARNS GREETING HARRIET BEECHER STOWE
State Archives of Florida
Rc00551

8   THE GROVE
State Archives of Florida
PR12068

9   AFRICAN AMERICAN PEOPLE AT MARKET
State Archives of Florida
Rc04819

10   INSPECTION TEAM WITH ENGINE #28
State Archives of Florida
Ha00028

11   SCENE IN GOVERNOR BLOXHAM'S PARLOR
State Archives of Florida
Gv000424

12   F. H. FLAGG HOME
State Archives of Florida
PR12168

13   FLORIDA'S 14TH GOVERNOR E. A. PERRY
State Archives of Florida
Rc00629

14   WEST FLORIDA SEMINARY BUILDING
State Archives of Florida
Rc04562

15   FLORIDA SENATE
State Archives of Florida
Rc12194

16   BOYS AND CREW WITH FLORIDA RAILWAY
State Archives of Florida
HA00076

17   NEW LEON HOTEL
State Archives of Florida
HA00058

18   FOX HUNTING GROUP
State Archives of Florida
Rc01983

19   FLORIDA LEGISLATURE
State Archives of Florida
Rc04337

20   EIGHT MEN WITH PENNY-FARTHING BICYCLES
State Archives of Florida
Rc00877

21   FOUR CHILDREN ON AN OX CART
State Archives of Florida
Rc03032

22   OFFICE OF THE WEEKLY FLORIDIAN
State Archives of Florida
HA00011

23   ALVAN S. HARPER AND HIS PONY
State Archives of Florida
HA00221

24 **BROKAW-MCDOUGALL HOUSE**
State Archives of Florida
Rc04342

25 **LABORERS BOILING CANE SYRUP**
State Archives of Florida
HA00073

26 **SAWMILL**
State Archives of Florida
Ha00018

27 **STREET SCENE**
State Archives of Florida
PR12401

28 **WINTHROP CHILDREN ON HORSEBACK WITH THE MERRITS**
State Archives of Florida
Ha00223

29 **ON PARK AVENUE**
State Archives of Florida
PR12413

30 **JOHN D. CAY**
State Archives of Florida
Rc13243

31 **COLLEGE AVENUE**
State Archives of Florida
PR12412

32 **BROWN HOUSE**
State Archives of Florida
PR11994

33 **CHILDREN IN YARD**
State Archives of Florida
Rc04871

34 **FOWLERS WITH GROUP**
State Archives of Florida
Rc03248

35 **THE LEON**
State Archives of Florida
Rc06725

36 **BALL BROS. & DEMILLY GENERAL STORE**
State Archives of Florida
Rc02518

37 **TALLAHASSEE RAILROAD COMPANY'S MULE-DRAWN TROLLEY**
State Archives of Florida
Rc08644

38 **STORES ON WEST SIDE OF MONROE**
State Archives of Florida
Rc06723

39 **MEN AND STATE TREASURER JAMES B. WHITFIELD**
State Archives of Florida
Rc03243

40 **CYCLISTS**
State Archives of Florida
N029579

41 **ALVAN S. HARPER**
State Archives of Florida
Rc02417

42 **COLLEGE HALL AT THE FLORIDA STATE COLLEGE FOR WOMEN**
State Archives of Florida
PR13013

43 **DIRTY SMITH**
State Archives of Florida
Rc00026

44 **WANISH CIGAR FACTORY**
State Archives of Florida
Rc04813

45 **WEST FLORIDA SEMINARY FOOTBALL TEAM**
State Archives of Florida
N044028

46 **WILLIAM HODGES' OFFICE**
State Archives of Florida
Rc02917

47 **FROZEN FOUNTAIN ON CAPITOL GROUNDS**
State Archives of Florida
Rc00730

48 **GEORGIA, FLORIDA & ALABAMA RAILWAY**
State Archives of Florida
N039185

50 **SCHOOL OF THE SOUTH**
State Archives of Florida
N042788

51 **HORSE-DRAWN BUGGY**
State Archives of Florida
Rc13806

52 **DEALERSHIP OF FORD OVERLAND AUTOMOBILES**
State Archives of Florida
Rc12203

53 **FLORIDA'S 18TH GOVERNOR, WILLIAM S. JENNINGS**
State Archives of Florida
Rc08264

54 **CAPITAL CITY BANK**
State Archives of Florida
Rc02558

55 **CONFEDERATE VETERANS**
State Archives of Florida
Rc11577

56 **T. B. BYRD GROCERY STORE**
State Archives of Florida
Rc09795

57 **FIREMEN**
State Archives of Florida
Rc03440

58 **ZACH FENN, PHELPS WILSON, AND JOHN P. BROWN IN A 1903 PANHARD**
State Archives of Florida
Rc10294

59 **FLORIDA COLLEGE GRADUATES**
State Archives of Florida
Rc01138

60 **PARKER BROTHERS**
State Archives of Florida
Rc00556

61 **GOVERNOR NAPOLEON B. BROWARD**
State Archives of Florida
Gv000423b

62 **DINNER**
State Archives of
Florida
Rc03074

63 **TURPENTINE STILL**
State Archives of
Florida
PR12641

64 **F.S.C. FOOTBALL**
State Archives of
Florida
Rc01140

65 **THE BREEZE HOTEL**
State Archives of
Florida
Rc10829

66 **BOY SCOUT TROOP**
State Archives of
Florida
PR11445

67 **FORMER GOVERNOR
WILLIAM D.
BLOXHAM**
State Archives of
Florida
Gv002547

68 **LEON ACADEMY
GIRLS BASKETBALL
TEAM**
State Archives of
Florida
N043226

69 **GOODWOOD**
State Archives of
Florida
pr12117

70 **MONROE STREET**
State Archives of
Florida
Rc04132

71 **JOHN P. BROWN
DRIVING MR. LEWIS**
State Archives of
Florida
Rc10298

72 **AVIATION**
State Archives of
Florida
Rc02915

74 **SHOT PUTTING AT
FIELD DAY**
State Archives of
Florida
N046546

75 **JAMES E. BOWDOIN**
State Archives of
Florida
Rc07200

76 **FLOAT IN CENTENNIAL
PARADE**
State Archives of
Florida
N047417

77 **FIREFIGHTERS AND
CHILD**
State Archives of
Florida
Rc03447

78 **MIDDLE FLORIDA ICE
COMPANY**
State Archives of
Florida
Rc12144

79 **F.S.C.W. STUDENTS**
State Archives of
Florida
Rc01237

80 **THE CARNEGIE
LIBRARY**
State Archives of
Florida
PR12683

81 **CELEBRATION**
State Archives of
Florida
n046315

82 **LEON HIGH SCHOOL
FOOTBALL TEAM**
State Archives of
Florida
N047874

83 **FLORIDA'S GOVERNOR
JOHN W. MARTIN**
State Archives of
Florida
GV008238

84 **SUPREME COURT**
State Archives of
Florida
Pc4194

85 **BAPTIST CHURCH**
State Archives of
Florida
Pc4157

86 **MASONIC BUILDING**
State Archives of
Florida
Pc4159

87 **DALE MABRY
MUNICIPAL AIRPORT**
State Archives of
Florida
Rc12119

88 **VENETIA RESTAURANT
AND HOTEL**
State Archives of
Florida
PR12388

89 **FLORIDA'S 25TH
GOVERNOR DOYLE E.
CARLTON**
State Archives of
Florida
Rc13392

90 **GYMNASIUM BUILDING**
State Archives of
Florida
PR12676

91 **STREET SCENE**
State Archives of
Florida
N045877

92 **AUTOMOBILES**
State Archives of
Florida
Rc20608

93 **J. L. JORDAN
GROCERIES**
State Archives of
Florida
Rc12167

94 **STREET SCENE**
State Archives of
Florida
N045874

95 **CHRISTENING OF THE
TALLAHASSEE FLYER
TRAIN**
State Archives of
Florida
GV008253

96 **COLLEGE AVENUE**
State Archives of
Florida
N043283

97 **INAUGURATION**
State Archives of
Florida
GV013308

98 **POLICE DEPARTMENT**
State Archives of
Florida
Rc03461

99 **FIRST EASTERN
AIRLINES FLIGHT**
State Archives of
Florida
Rc00691

100 **DOVE SHOOT**
State Archives of
Florida
N047124

101 **MAY PARTY**
State Archives of
Florida
PR11510

102 **GREEN DERBY**
State Archives of
Florida
PR11098

103 **FSCW's Astronomy Club**
State Archives of Florida
Rc01316

104 **Airplanes "on the line"**
State Archives of Florida
N044866

106 **Luella Knott**
State Archives of Florida
N043089

107 **Couples Say Goodnight**
State Archives of Florida
RC01339

108 **Ivan Munroe**
State Archives of Florida
N042097

109 **National Airlines Airplane**
State Archives of Florida
Gr0596

110 **Lee Hall at Florida A&M**
State Archives of Florida
c007751

111 **Monroe Street**
State Archives of Florida
RK0198

112 **Florida Governor Millard Caldwell**
State Archives of Florida
PT00233

113 **Southeastern Telephone Company Traffic Operating Room**
State Archives of Florida
Rc06641

114 **Seven Seas Restaurant**
State Archives of Florida
Rc09766

115 **Gulf Life Insurance Co.**
State Archives of Florida
Gr1282

116 **1953 Florida State University**
State Archives of Florida
Rck00095

117 **Police Destroying Confiscated Liquor**
State Archives of Florida
Rc12859

118 **Auction**
State Archives of Florida
Rc00560

119 **The Mecca**
State Archives of Florida
Rc01084

120 **Fire**
State Archives of Florida
N043180

121 **McClay Gardens**
State Archives of Florida
GR0852

122 **Governor Collins**
State Archives of Florida
c020348

123 **Governor's Mansion**
State Archives of Florida
c029066

124 **FSU Students**
State Archives of Florida
Rc06635

125 **Florida A&M Students**
State Archives of Florida
Rc12419

126 **Civil Rights**
State Archives of Florida
Rc12396-7E

127 **New Diet**
State Archives of Florida
C035240

128 **Business District**
State Archives of Florida
Rc06721

129 **Seminole Indians**
State Archives of Florida
Rc11826

130 **Governor and Mrs. Haydon Burns**
State Archives of Florida
GV036091

131 **Governor Claude Kirk at FSU**
State Archives of Florida
C65000-63

Printed in the USA
CPSIA information can be obtained
at www.ICGtesting.com
JSHW072022140824
68134JS00042B/3747